CPSIA information can be obtained
at www.ICGtesting.com
Printed in the USA
BVHW04s0923131018
530038BV00004B/4/P